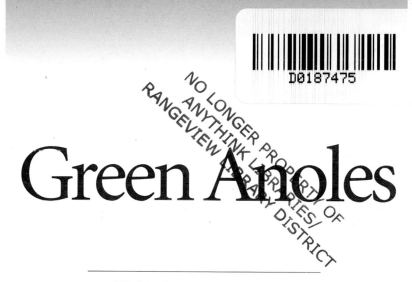

Green Anoles

FROM THE EXPERTS AT
ADVANCED VIVARIUM SYSTEMS™

By Philippe de Vosjoli

THE HERPETOCULTURAL LIBRARY®
Advanced Vivarium Systems™
Laguna Hills, California

Kristin Mehus-Roe, *editor*
Amy Fox, *project manager*
Nick Clemente, *special consultant*
Suzy Gehrls, *production manager*
Designed by Michael Vincent Capozzi
Rachel Rice, *indexer*

Cover photo courtesy of ©R. D. Bartlett
The photographs and illustrations in this book are courtesy of: Philippe de Vosjoli, pp.
5, 17, 33, 38 top, 56; Zig Leszczynski, pp. 7, 27, 29 top, 53; John Tashjian, pp. 8, 49 center
and bottom, 40 center and bottom; Jim Bridges, pp. 9, 41, 42, 47, 49 top, 52; Chris Estep,
pp. 10, 11, 28, 31, 36, 37, 44; John C. Tyson, pp. 14, 29 bottom; Bill Love, p. 15; Glen
Warren, p. 16; R.D. Bartlett, pp. 19, 43, 46; Vern French, pp. 21 top and bottom, 24, 57,
58; Eric Suchman, pp. 23, 39, 40; Paul Freed, pp. 32, 38 bottom; and Tom Jones, p. 50
top.

LCCN: 96-183295
ISBN-10: 1-882770-65-X
ISBN-13: 978-1-882770-65-6

An Imprint of BowTie Press®
A Division of BowTie, Inc.
23172 Plaza Pointe Dr., Ste. 230
Laguna Hills, CA 92653
www.avsbooks.com
866-888-5526

We want to hear from you. What books would you like to see in the future? Please feel
free to write us with any comments on our AVS books.

Printed in Singapore
15 14 13 12 11 10 09 08   5 6 7 8 9 10

CONTENTS

INTRODUCTION

For many of us in herpetoculture, green anoles have become such common pet trade fare that we barely notice them in stores or individual collections. Indeed, these neat little lizards have in their own way become the reptilian counterpart of the goldfish in the aquarium trade: the inexpensive first reptile that we buy our children when they insist on owning a pet.

Many of us forget that green anoles also provided our very first introduction to the class Reptilia and to reptilian consciousness. When we were children, something about that small lizard with those intense little black eyes was totally endearing and captivating, particularly when associated with stories about these lizards—popularly called "chameleons" in the pet trade—changing color. Of course, for children, one of the great features of anoles is that they are so tiny and harmless in appearance parents who would categorically refuse to allow their children to keep a snake or larger lizard usually give in to buying a green anole. After that first step, it is quite a bit easier to convince parents to let children keep another kind of reptile. This is the steppingstone strategy to becoming a herpetoculturist.

Until recently, green anoles suffered from a cheap-pet stigma. Just like goldfish, green anoles have frequently been marketed as creatures that could survive in the inexpensive setups they were often sold with—the reptile trade's version of the goldfish bowl: the mini-plastic terrarium. As for food, many retailers used to simply state that a few mealworms offered twice a week would keep the little buggers alive. All of this misinformation on anole care was in line with an antiquated pet marketing philosophy that preyed on the fact that many consumers wouldn't give much thought to spending $10 or $15 for a cheap pet and its setup. If the animal died, it could be replaced for another couple of bucks. Fortunately, the current trend among pet stores and reptile dealers is to advocate a more responsible philosophy of reptile care than the disposable animal and cheap setup quick-sales strategy that was once so widespread.

This book presents herpetoculture guidelines in line with the current philosophical trend toward responsible herpetoculture. The result, as I hope will be demonstrated by the information and photographs gathered for this book, is an enlightening glimpse into a dimension of the natural world where reptiles still rule: enacting ritual battles for territory, overpowering prey, and casting dragon spells that entrap careless humans into a lifelong fascination.

A male green anole eats the shed skin off its toes. Notice that green anoles don't mimic the coloration of their surroundings.

CHAPTER 1:

THE GREEN ANOLE AS A PET

Green anoles make great pets but they are not like dogs and cats. Anoles are best left in their cages to be observed, as they are easily stressed by handling. Like tropical fish, the fun of keeping an anole is in watching it in a beautiful, naturalistic vivarium.

Although there is a small anole harness sometimes offered in the pet trade, anoles for the most part are small and, at times, flighty lizards that are best observed rather than taken out and handled. If you want a pet lizard that can occasionally be handled, consider an Australian bearded dragon *(Pogona vitticeps)* or a blue-tongue skink *(Tiliqua scincoides)*. Both of these species are now bred in some numbers in the United States. Leopard geckos *(Eublepharis macularius)*, which are relatively inexpensive compared to the aforementioned species, are also much more suitable for handling than green anoles. Tame green iguanas *(Iguana iguana)* can also be handled, as can a number of other medium to large lizards, such as Sudan plated lizards *(Gerrhosaurus major)*.

Anoles fare best if you avoid handling them.

CHAPTER 2:

GENERAL INFORMATION

What are anoles? Anole is the common name given to a large group of small-sized to medium-sized New World lizards in the family Polychridae, most of them in the genus *Anolis*. They are characterized by an elongated form, a relatively long and laterally compressed tail, subdigital lamellae (toe pads), and an extensible throat structure called a dewlap. Most are semi-arboreal or arboreal (tree dwelling or shrub dwelling). All are primarily insectivorous, although some will eat soft fruit and the larger forms occasionally feed on small vertebrates. They are among the most colorful of New World lizards and, with nearly four hundred species, show a diversity of color and pattern even greater than is found in Malagasy day geckos.

Besides the members of the genus Anolis and its subgenera, anoles include the Andesian anoles (Phenacosaurus) and the cryptic ground-dwelling Chamaelinorops barbouri.

The Hispaniolan giant anole *(Anolis ricordi)* is an impressive species that was at one time imported in small numbers from Haiti.

A Martinique spotted anole *(Anolis roquet sumus)* displays its dewlap.

Almost all of the anoles in the pet trade are wild caught.

What's in a Name?

The correct popular name for the so-called American chameleon of the pet trade is green anole. Anoles are not chameleons; rather, all anoles are members of the genus *Anolis* of which there are more than two hundred species. *Anolis* is now considered to be in the New World family Polychridae. The true chameleons are Old World lizards that belong to the family Chamaeleonidae. The scientific name of the green anole is *Anolis carolinensis*.

Distribution

Anolis carolinensis is the only species of anole native to the mainland United States. The green anole is found from North Carolina south to the Florida Keys and west to southeast Oklahoma and central Texas. It has been introduced in several areas, including Hawaii. All other anole species found in south Florida were introduced.

Size

The total length of adults ranges from 5 to 8 inches, but only males are likely to exceed 6 inches. The tail accounts for nearly two-thirds of the total length. Hatchlings have a total length of 2⅟₁₆ to 2⅝ inches.

Growth Rate

Green anoles, if maintained properly, grow from hatchling to small adult size in six to eight months.

Longevity

In the wild, green anoles typically live less than two and a half years. In captivity, when properly cared for, green anoles have lived up to eight years, although typical lifespan is three to six years. Unfortunately, anoles sold in the pet trade seldom live for more than a year because they are generally miscared for and neglected due to owner ignorance about proper husbandry.

Dewlaps

Dewlaps are sometimes called throat fans and are used for communication related to breeding and territoriality. During territorial displays, males will perform brief, repeated extensions of the dewlaps. In most green anoles sold in the pet trade, which frequently originate from Louisiana, the dewlaps are pink. In green anoles from south Florida, the dewlaps may vary from whites to pinks to pastel blues and purples.

A male and a female green anole prepare to mate. Notice the dewlap of the displaying male and the whitish mid-dorsal line of the female.

Sexing

Male anoles eventually grow larger than females. The heads of males become proportionately larger with age, and their dewlaps also grow larger than females'. Most females retain a white to grayish mid-dorsal line (line down the back) more prominent than when present in males (most males lack a mid-dorsal line). If in doubt, the most noticeable difference is the prominent hemipenal (male sex organ) bulge clearly visible in older males at the base of the tail.

Color Change

There is a popular misconception that anoles change color to match their surroundings. In fact, these lizards have a rather limited repertoire of color change and from little to none involving pattern change. Anoles change coloration to thermoregulate (regulate their body temperature), becoming darker when they are cold and lighter when they are too warm. They also change color as a means to express emotion, such as during territorial displays. At night when sleeping, green anoles adopt a light nocturnal coloration. This color change makes them easily visible when collecting this species with the aid of a flashlight.

Shown is a rare blue morph of the green anole. This attractive color morph is highly sought by collectors and warrants captive propagation.

The most remarkable color changes in vertebrates occur in some of the true chameleons, some of which rank among the most beautiful of all animals.

Morphs

Occasionally, pastel blue specimens of green anoles are collected and offered in the trade. These blue anoles, which are apparently axanthic animals (lacking yellow pigment), are few and far between. According to one anole distributor in Louisiana, there is one blue anole brought in by collectors per at least twenty thousand specimens. With some efforts in selective breeding, more specimens could become available in the future. As could be expected, these blue anoles fetch high prices, often $100 or more at the retail level. Other color mutations are very occasionally found in green anoles, but few are as attractive as the pastel blue.

CHAPTER 3:
SELECTING HEALTHY GREEN ANOLES

The selection of initially healthy animals is critical to the long-term success of maintaining green anoles in captivity. The following guidelines will help you select potentially healthy animals:

- Select animals that are of small to medium size. Avoid very large animals, as they may be old and thus less likely to live for long. Older animals may also be heavily parasitized and often do not acclimate as well to captivity.
- Select animals with rounded bodies and rounded tails. Avoid animals in which the hip bones or vertebral processes are prominent and clearly visible through the skin.
- The eyes of healthy anoles are alert and rounded. Avoid animals with sunken or half-closed eyes.
- Select active animals. The "lazy" anole that just sits there in your hand, appearing nearly tame, is probably sick and incapable of behaving like a healthy anole.
- While holding the animal in your hand, turn it upside down and inspect the vent (opening to the cloaca, the common urinary, generative, and intestinal channel) and check for smeared, watery stools or dried diarrhea. Avoid animals with these symptoms.
- Don't think for a second you will be able to save the poor sick anole you see in a store. Sick anoles usually die.

CHAPTER 4:

HOUSING

On Keeping Anole Groups

As a general rule, it is recommended to keep anoles either singly or in groups consisting of one male and one or more females, but this is a broad guideline. When green anoles are kept under proper conditions where they are not overcrowded, males kept together will establish territories, demonstrate territorial displays, and chase or fight each other, particularly during the breeding season. At that time, weaker males may get injured. There will also be competition during feeding; larger animals will intimidate smaller, weaker animals.

Whether mixing groups of several males and females will work in the long run depends on a number of factors including the type of anole species, the number of anoles kept together, the size of the vivarium, and the design and landscaping of the vivarium. For example, in the overcrowded conditions in which anoles are maintained at

Many large distributors make concerted efforts to provide adequate conditions for their animals.

A male anole performs aggressive display. Most anoles are highly territorial and should be carefully monitored when maintained in groups.

large-scale animal dealers, the conditions usually don't allow for the establishment of territories and serious fights are minimal. When keeping anoles in a home vivarium, breaking up the space in a vivarium with tall plants or rocks and wood can allow for enough visual isolation between males that with certain species several can safely be kept together. This is an area where one will have to experiment with respective species.

Enclosures

Popular enclosures marketed for keeping green anoles are relatively small plastic terraria with plastic lids. These plastic terraria are useful for the maintenance of a number of other animals but they are inadequate and unsuitable for the long-term maintenance of green anoles. Over a period of a few weeks or months, the great majority of anoles kept in these containers die. Keeping anoles in these enclosures is tantamount to keeping a dog in a small kennel with little light, inadequate heat, and inadequate stimulation. The new larger versions of plastic terraria (10 gallons or more) provide adequate space, but the plastic molded tops create problems in terms of being able to safely provide adequate heat and light. An incandescent bulb in a metal reflector can melt the top. Any herpetoculturist who cares about the welfare of these lizards will not keep them in mini plastic terraria. The best enclosures for keeping green anoles are all-glass tanks with screen tops.

The minimum size for keeping one to two green anoles should be a standard 10-gallon aquarium/vivarium (20-inches-long by 12-inches-high by 10-inches-wide) with a standard 20-gallon container (24-inches-long by 16-inches-high by 12-inches-wide) being even more desirable. If more than a trio of these animals is to be kept together, then a larger size is recommended. If you want to keep several anoles or a variety of plant and animal life, then bigger is better. The best vivaria that the author has seen for anoles were 100-gallon, 6-foot-long, all-glass tanks. One of these contained a fascinating array of plant and animal life, including five species of lizards, three species of frogs, and one species of newt. A well-designed vivarium can be as attractive and as captivating as a tropical fish aquarium.

Any enclosure for keeping green anoles should have a securely fitted screen cover. Green anoles can climb glass and will readily escape from any uncovered enclosure.

Designing a Basic Vivarium

Unfortunately, for many people green anoles are simply cheap pets for their children and they are unwilling to spend the money required for the design of a naturalistic

Shown is a basic setup for keeping green anoles.

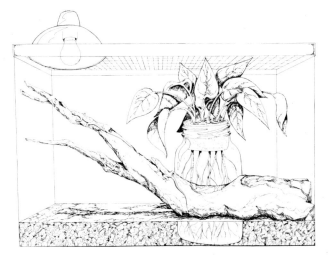

vivarium. However, it still costs several times the price of an anole to purchase even the minimum amount of supplies for successful long-term maintenance. This is another way in which keeping lizards in a vivarium is no different than keeping tropical fish. The basic cost of an aquarium exceeds many times over the cost of most of the fish it holds. The following are the minimum design requirements for a basic vivarium for the maintenance of green anoles.

A pothos plant adds appeal to an anole setup, even in a simply designed 10-gallon vivarium.

Minimum Enclosure
A 10-gallon, all-glass tank with screen top.

Lighting
An incandescent bulb in a reflector-type fixture should be placed at one end of the vivarium to provide heat. The wattage of the bulb required depends on the air temperature of the room where the vivarium is maintained. For a 10-gallon vivarium, a 40- to 60-watt bulb is usually adequate for an enclosure with an uncovered screen top maintained at a room temperature of 70-74° F. Enclosures that have a partially covered top, either with glass or Plexiglas, require a lower wattage bulb or the vivarium will overheat. A thermometer should always be used to adjust

the vivarium temperature. It should read 85–90° F when measured at the level of the branches closest to the light. At ground level at the distance farthest from the lights, the temperature should be considerably cooler. Do not place an incandescent bulb directly over live plants or you stand a good chance of burning the leaves.

Note: A spotlight in a reflector over a smaller vivarium will not allow for a range of heat gradients and will overheat reptiles.

Ground Medium

An attractive ground medium is seedling or small grade orchid bark. Specialized reptile stores and nurseries sell both of these. Many pet stores will recommend smooth aquarium pea gravel, which also works. A barely moistened peat moss based potting soil without perlite is also highly recommended for keeping anoles. However, sand should not be used as a ground medium as anoles can ingest it, causing intestinal blockages.

Landscaping

Anoles are arboreal to semiarboreal lizards that require suitable climbing areas. To accommodate these behaviors place some branches of select wood, with diameters equal to or slightly greater than the width of your lizards, diagonally across the vivarium. You can also place thin pieces of cork bark diagonally across the vivarium. A pot of pothos vine *(Scindapsus aureus)*, obtainable in most nurseries, plant stores, or plant sections in supermarkets, can be grown in the vivarium in two ways: hydroponically in a concealed jar of water or planted directly in the ground medium. To grow pothos hydroponically, carefully remove a rooted section of pothos from a pot and rinse the roots of all soil. Then place the section(s), roots first, in a jar of water. Cover the opening with a section of foam rubber. In time, the pothos will form water roots adapted to growing in water. An alternative to using sections with roots is to use stem cuttings. They too will produce water roots in due time. If you spread some of the stems onto the branches,

Provide plants
and branches
for your anole
to climb and
perch on.

the leaves of the plant will provide a surface on which
anoles can climb and from which they can drink droplets
of water. The plant will also help raise the relative humidity
in the vivarium.

A Hand Sprayer

Use purified water in a hand sprayer to mist plant leaves
and the walls of the tank daily. If you simply use regular tap
water, you will probably end up with hard-to-remove and
unsightly mineral deposits on the sides of your tank as well
as on the leaves of plants.

Note

The above are the minimum requirements for maintaining
green anoles. For maintaining the other species of amphibi-

ans and reptiles compatible with green anoles, a larger enclosure and additional heat in the form of a subtank heater should be included. For most companion species, a shallow water container needs to be included.

Designing a Naturalistic Vivarium

The most attractive and interesting vivaria for keeping small reptiles and amphibians are naturalistic vivaria that

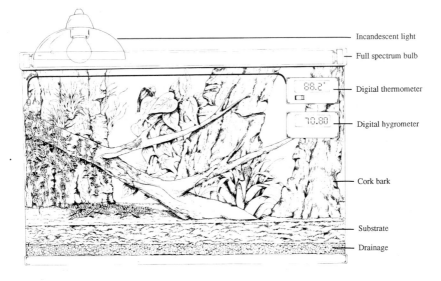

Incandescent light

Full spectrum bulb

88.2° Digital thermometer

70.80 Digital hygrometer

Cork bark

Substrate

Drainage

simulate essential aspects of an animal's habitat in combination with a varied landscape design and a variety of ornamental plants. When planning the design of these vivaria, as much emphasis is placed on the plant species and landscape features as on the species of animals selected. The end result can be vivaria whose aesthetic impact will equal that of the best-designed tropical fish aquaria.

Enclosure

The bare minimum enclosure size for creating a naturalistic vivarium is a standard 20-gallon tank, although larger sizes are preferable. As a general rule, the larger the vivarium, the greater the possibilities of incorporating a varied and interesting design.

A 6-foot-long naturalistic vivarium designed by Susan Jones and Vern French decorates an apartment.

Lighting

For the welfare of plants and the psychological welfare of the animals, fluorescent full-spectrum reptile bulbs should be placed running the length of the vivarium. Ideally, at least two bulbs should be used. In large vivaria, and depending on the plants used, some herpetoculturists use banks of four bulbs. These bulbs are the key to maintaining attractive naturalistic vivaria. They provide the lighting that makes plants thrive and orchids bloom. For many lizards the UV-A (a lower frequency of ultraviolet radiation) generated by these bulbs has psychological benefits that will increase the probability of long term

This vivarium shows various bromeliads, rosary vine, and a number of anole species. The vivarium is lit by a bank of four 6-foot Vita Lite bulbs and two small incandescent spotlights.

survival and possibly stimulate feeding and breeding. During most of the year, the lights should be set on a timer so that they remain on fourteen hours a day. In the winter, the light schedule should be cut back to ten hours a day particularly if you are interested in breeding the animals. Use a plug-in timer.

Ground Medium

At least two layers of substrata are required when designing a naturalistic vivarium. On the bottom of the vivarium, a 1- to 1½-inch layer of coarse gravel should be placed as a drainage layer. Above that, spread a 2- to 3-inch layer of a sandy (add 10 percent sand) peat-based potting soil. Herpetoculturists will often mix in about 10 percent seedling orchid bark to increase drainage. Do not use commercial potting soils that contain perlite or polystyrene foam. The foam will rise to the surface when the soil is watered and can be ingested by lizards.

Some herpetoculturists place a layer of small-grade orchid bark on parts of the surface of the vivarium after planting and landscaping the vivarium. The end result when viewed from the side is a two- or three-layered substratum, which makes it easy to determine whether the soil has been suitably watered or not. As the soil dries out, the moisture level seen from the side will diminish from the top of the soil down. If too much water is applied, the excess water will be seen accumulating in the drainage layer.

Landscaping

Interesting vivaria are those that have a varied topography. The topography can be designed by using rocks or driftwood to create layers within the vivarium. Other materials that work are pieces of cork or dried-out stumps with root bases emerging from the bottom.

Plants for Anole Vivaria

One cannot readily appreciate the behaviors of green anoles without providing plants on which the animals can display their relatively wide range of behaviors. One of the most easily maintained and recommended of vivarium plants is pothos. Other plants also work well in anole vivaria.
- *Snakeplants (Sansevieria sp.):* Good choices are: The birdsnest sansevieria (S. t. "Hahnii"), the common snakeplant (S. t. trifasciata), Sansevieria "Moonshine," and (Sansevieria metallica). The latter has beautiful

This naturalistic tropical vivarium was designed by the author and Eric Suchman for the Forgotten Forest, a now-defunct store that sold plants and animals.

leaves and is obtainable by mail order from nurseries that specialize in succulents.

There are many other species of suitable sansevierias, several of which have odd-shaped cylindrical and grooved leaves. Their hardiness and unusual forms and patterns make them among the most interesting plants for herpetoculturists but finding the odd species will take some work, such as looking in horticulture magazines and writing specialty succulent nurseries for their catalogs.

- *Bromeliads:* Many species of bromeliads (members of the pineapple family) do well in a vivarium with moderately good light (at least two fluorescent bulbs no more than 16 inches from the leaf surfaces) and good drainage (up to 20 percent orchid bark in the soil medium). Good choices are neoregelias, guzmanias, vriesias, and, at ground level, the various earth stars (Cryptanthus spp.). Some of the cultivars such as C. zonatus can add beautiful color and patterning in the landscaping of the vivarium. In a large vivarium with banks of four fluorescent bulbs or more, some of the epiphytic tillandsias can be grown on cork bark placed in close proximity to the lights. As a general rule, bromeliads with spiny leaf edges should not be used with amphibians and reptiles because of the possible risk of injuries.
- *Orchids:* A good candidate for larger tropical vivaria with good drainage and adequate lighting is the terres-

trial jewel orchid (Haemaria discolor), with its beautiful velvety maroon leaves streaked in gold. Moth orchids (Phalaenopsis spp.), Dendrobiums, and Epidendrums, as well as a variety of small epiphytic orchids, can be grown in an anole vivarium. Moth orchids or other orchids that are grown in pots are best placed in their pots within the vivarium. The pot can be buried in the substratum or concealed with sections of wood or stone. Epiphytic orchids should be attached to cork bark or wood at a close distance from fluorescent full spectrum lights. There's a lot of room for experimentation here and many possible species of orchids to choose from.

- *Vines:* With good lighting and good drainage, the rosary vine (Ceropegia woodii) grows well and can be sprawled across branches for an attractive effect. In larger vivaria, you can use smaller species of philodendron such as the popular heartleaf philodendron (Philodendron corda-

An anole lies on a hibiscus. These are difficult to grow in a vivarium, but anoles like to climb on them.

tum). As a ground cover, you can use creeping fig (Ficus pumila) but you must prune it regularly or it will become too dense and problematic. With good lighting, many other vines can successfully grow in the vivarium, including other philodendrons (Philodendron spp.), passion vines (Passiflora spp.), several types of morning glories (Ipomoea spp.), and some grape relatives (Cissus spp. and Parthenocissus spp.).

All of the above mentioned plants have been tested by the author over several years with anoles and will survive in vivaria that include strong light, moderately high relative humidity, and adequate ventilation.

Heating

In tropical vivaria, provide two types of heating.

- *Subtank Heating:* You can use a below-ground or sub-tank heating system, such as nursery soil heating cables or one of the subtank heating devices currently available in the reptile trade. With the use of a rheostat, which controls the electrical current, some of the sub-tank heating devices sold by reptile dealers can even be adjusted. Take care, however, to follow the manufacturer's instructions as to the safe use of these devices to prevent the risk of fire or cracking the bottom of the glass enclosure.
- *Basking Light:* Incandescent bulbs or small spotlights should be placed over select basking areas, such as sections of cork bark or branches, so that the temperature measures 85–90° F at the basking areas closest to the basking light. The wattage required depends on the size of the enclosure and the distance from basking sites. The daytime air temperature in the vivarium at the furthest end from the basking sites should be 75–86° F. Place at least one thermometer in the vivarium, preferably near a basking site. One of the best thermometers for these vivaria is a digital readout thermometer with an outdoor sensor, which you can find in most electronic supply stores. These thermometers allow for a continuous readout from a specific location in the vivarium.

For green anoles, daytime air temperatures in the vivarium should be 75–86° F. The temperature at the basking sites closest to incandescent bulbs or spotlights should be 85–90° F. At night, the temperature can safely drop into the upper 60s and even considerably cooler in the winter.

For tropical anoles, the night temperature should not drop below 72° F.

Relative Humidity

Anoles fare best in vivaria with moderate to high relative humidity, 50 percent or greater (certain tropical species may require at least 80 percent to fare well). Humidity can be measured with a hygrometer—inexpensive versions of these humidity gauges are now sold in the pet trade. With live plants that receive regular daily misting, proper humidity levels can be readily achieved. However, in unusually dry climates, you may need to partially cover the vivarium screen with a section of clear Plexiglas. A small, cool-air humidifier in a room is useful, particularly if you are maintaining several vivaria in the same room.

Ventilation

In any vivarium containing green anoles or any of the other animals mentioned in the compatible species section at the end of this book, it is essential that the vivarium have good ventilation. Most amphibians and reptiles (there are a few exceptions) eventually die if maintained in a mostly covered vivarium with poor ventilation, saturated air humidity, and high condensation levels. To successfully maintain anoles and other animals in this type of setup the screen top should be uncovered with no obstacle to air flow. Only in unusually dry climates should a small section of the screen top (less than one-third of the cover surface) be covered to reduce the evaporation rate within the vivarium. Under most circumstances, with daily misting and regular watering, adequate relative air humidity is easily maintained within the vivarium.

Caretakers should provide adequate humidity through misting and the use of plants.

Vivarium Alternatives

Custom-made screen or small wire-mesh cages can be practical for pet stores wishing to keep large numbers of anoles on hand. Branches and a few potted plants provide all the basic landscaping necessary. You can use screened cages but you will lose some visibility, as well as a great deal of display appeal. You will also have to take extra care to ensure adequate relative humidity. The use of live plants and misting several times a day is recommended.

CHAPTER 5:

DIET

Insect Prey

The most readily available and recommended food for green anoles is commercially raised crickets. Feed adult green anoles two- to three-week-old crickets. Many pet stores sell five- to six-week-old crickets that are too large for this species. If you really care, you will buy the right size crickets to feed your anoles.

Mealworms are not a recommended food for green anoles unless you raise these worms at home, in which case smaller mealworms, $\frac{1}{16}$ of an inch thick, can be used as an occasional component of the diet. Just molted "white" mealworms with a soft exoskeleton are also a suitable food for adult anoles. The problem with standard mealworms is

Green anoles in a reptile store rush to grab supplemented two- to three-week-old crickets placed in a plastic deli container to reduce dispersal rate.

that their chitinous exoskeleton is difficult to digest and also too thick for anoles to readily tear while chewing. A common occurrence is for anoles to grab and swallow a whole large mealworm only to regurgitate it a day or two later.

Small wax worms, the caterpillars of the wax moth (*Galleria mellonella*) are recommended in small quantities to diversify their diet. If the caterpillars are allowed to pupate (which they will if maintained at warmer temperatures), the resulting moths will be relished by anoles.

A favorite food of anoles is flies, which can be offered for variety but should never make up an anole's primary diet,

Gut load crickets and mealworms before offering them to your anole.

unless you want to gut load the flies (feed them prior to offering to your anoles) on a nutritious diet such as moist dog food or lean meat with multivitamins. To obtain flies, the best source is commercially bred fly larvae (now available in many specialized reptile stores) raised on a relatively hygienic vegetarian diet such as cornmeal. At warm temperatures, the larvae will pupate. The pupae can then be placed in a small container inside the vivarium and the flies allowed to emerge.

Preparing Insects

Commercially raised insects tend to lose weight as well as nutritional value during shipping and during storage in a pet store. In addition, the nutritional quality of diets fed to crickets is often inadequate to provide proper nutrition to reptiles. Indeed, a significant amount of the nutritional qualities of insects are the result of dietary matter stored in their guts.

Thus, crickets and mealworms should be gut-loaded with nutrients prior to feeding them to green anoles. Do this by placing the crickets in a small plastic terrarium for twelve to twenty-four hours and offering them either chicken mash, ground rodent chow, high-quality tropical fish flakes, or high-protein flaked baby cereal. As a source of water and vitamin C, offer the crickets slices of orange. As a source of beta-carotene, alternate with some grated carrots. Offer the crickets to your anoles the next day. Some stores make an effort and nutrient-boost insects as a standard feeding procedure. Inquire as to the diet a store feeds its insect prey. Remember: every time a lizard eats, it also ingests the gut contents of its prey. A lizard is what its prey eats.

Multivitamin/Mineral Supplementation

Every other feeding (twice a week), supplement insects with a quality reptile or bird vitamin/mineral powder. This is done by adding a small amount of the powder in a jar, introducing the crickets, gently shaking the jar to coat the crickets with the mix, and introducing them in a feeding dish in the vivarium. A small porcelain feeding dish is recommended to prevent rapid dispersal of the crickets and the subsequent loss of vitamin/mineral coating.

Feeding Schedule

For an optimal feeding schedule, offer green anoles food every other day. Do not offer more crickets or food items than the lizards will eat at a sitting. Usually two or three appropriately sized food items are all that an anole requires to have its fill. Excess crickets simply dropped in a vivarium rapidly lose all vitamin/mineral coating. These loose insects will be eaten later as the anoles become hungry again. When you feed the anoles next time, they will not be as eager to feed on newly introduced food (they will be full from having eaten the stragglers) and a pattern of delayed feeding on unsupplemented crickets will occur. The end result can be vitamin-deficient lizards, so don't feed more than your lizards will eat at one sitting.

An economical way to supplement the diet of green anoles maintained in large numbers is to introduce peach baby food supplemented with a vitamin/mineral powder.

Water

Anoles do not readily drink from a bowl containing still water. They prefer to drink from droplets of water that reflect light. The easiest and most recommended method for providing water to anoles is to lightly spray their enclosure once or twice daily during the daytime. They will then lap droplets from leaves and the glass sides of the vivarium. Purified bottled water is recommended for this purpose or accumulations of minerals will quickly stain the glass of your vivarium and impair viewing.

Other methods include using a shallow container of water in which a section of aquarium tubing connected to an air pump has been placed. The bubbling water will create the light play that anoles use to recognize water. There is also an effective and simple passive drip system that can be used, consisting of placing a low-sided deli container (the type of small container used at a takeout restaurant) under an area with overhanging leaves inside the vivarium. Another deli container with a tiny hole at the bottom is placed outside of the vivarium on the area of the screen top just above the underlying container. Fill the upper container with water and it will drop water slowly one drop at a time, with drops striking the underlying leaves before landing in the lower container. The anoles will drink from the splattered droplets on the leaves.

CHAPTER 6:

DISEASES AND DISORDERS

Partially because of their small size, green anoles are difficult to treat, and, as a general rule, they usually die once they appear ill. Both the low cost of green anoles and their relative abundance have resulted in a lack of veterinary treatment of these animals when they are ill. The veterinary treatment of such small lizards costs many times the initial price of the animals and is frequently unsuccessful. In addition, the particular and rapid metabolism of small lizards often results in rapid decline when ill. The small size also makes the dosage and administration of medication difficult for herpeToculturists. Furthermore, the rapid rate of decline of small lizards seldom allows enough time for the medication to take effect. Thus, careful daily monitoring of small reptiles is important so that you will notice when their condition appears even slightly off. Efforts should be made to determine early on any possible diseases or environmental causes.

Anoles often adopt a mottled darkened coloration when they are dying.

Botflies

Parasitism by botfly larvae is a common cause of death of green anoles in the wild. Sometimes green anoles purchased from stores die as a result of botfly parasitism. The adult botfly lays eggs under the skin of an anole. After the eggs hatch, the maggots feed on the inside of the animal. Typically, an open sore appears on the anole, from which one or more botfly maggots are visible. These animals should be euthanized by placing them in a plastic deli cup with a cover and putting the cup in the freezer. Anoles parasitized with botfly larvae seldom survive.

Other Internal Parasites

These should not be of much concern to herpetoculturists unless their animals are eating but failing to gain or maintain weight. A fecal sample can be taken by a veterinarian if necessary. Administering wormers to green anoles may be problematic in group situations, for example, a newly imported group of anoles at a retail dealer. One method consists of placing all the anoles in a box. Weigh the box full of anoles, then weigh the box by itself and subtract the weight of the anoles—this will give the weight of the anole group. Then, wormer tablets, such as piperazine, are weighed to treat the entire group. Pulverize the tablets finely with a mortar and pestle. At the next feeding, place small crickets in a container with the pulverized wormer, shake to coat with the wormer, and feed to the group. The treatment should be repeated three times (once every seven to ten days). Other medications can be administered to anole groups or groups of other small lizards in this manner. Metronidazole (Flagyl) in pulverized form can be effectively administered to a group in the same manner for treatment of flagellate protozoans.

Respiratory Infections

In anoles, a puffed up appearance of the body and occasional mouth gaping followed by forced exhalations are characteristic symptoms of respiratory infections. Other associated symptoms include listlessness and loss of appetite.

Treatment

Increase cage temperature to 85–88° F with no drop at night. Administering antibiotics through a nebulizer can be useful when treating groups of animals. Other methods used by some herpetoculturists to treat groups of anoles include pulverizing an antibiotic such as tetracycline with a mortar and pestle and coating the food with the powder. Another method is to put an oral antibiotic in the water when misting. A veterinarian should be consulted to obtain the most effective antibiotic and to determine dosage when administering to a group of animals.

Gastroenteritis

Typical symptoms include runny stools, caked and smeared diarrhea around the vent area, loss of appetite, loss of weight, and listlessness. The only way to reliably diagnose the cause is to have a stool check performed by a veterinarian. Some herpetoculturists routinely treat these animals by administering metronidazole at a dosage of 75 mg/kg (0.075mg/g). This will treat animals with flagellate protozoans, a common cause of gastroenteritis in reptiles. In group situations, metronidazole can be finely pulverized and used to coat crickets or other insect food items. The treatment should be repeated in two weeks.

Some of the above methods for treating small reptiles may seem unprofessional and haphazard to veterinarians, however, the cost of veterinary treatment along with the high mortality rate for small lizards often precludes professional treatment. Although professional treatment is best, these methods can be effective for those owners unwilling to visit a veterinarian.

CHAPTER 7:

BREEDING

Because of their low cost and their relative abundance, herpetoculturists usually make no concentrated efforts to breed green anoles, although they will make efforts at propagating some of the more exotic and difficult-to-obtain *Anolis* species.

When properly maintained, green anoles will breed readily in a vivarium. For many herpetoculturists, this becomes apparent when a hatchling anole is suddenly seen moving about the vivarium.

A pair of green anoles mates.

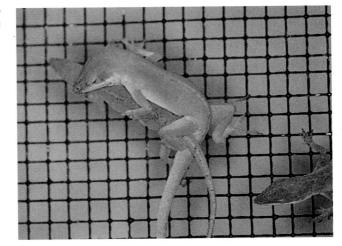

Breeding Season

In most anoles, breeding is triggered by longer photoperiods, so in the wild it begins in the spring when day length increases. In some tropical areas, anoles breed most of the year. In captivity, the breeding season can be initiated and extended by manipulating the photoperiod. A rest period of at least three months is recommended.

Optimal Conditions

To help induce breeding in green anoles, the photoperiod during the winter should be reduced to ten hours of daylight and fourteen hours of darkness for two months. At night, the temperature should be allowed to drop to as low as 60° F, although green anoles will tolerate temperatures into the 40s for brief periods without harm. The daytime temperature during this cooling period should be a few degrees cooler. Anoles will not feed as much or as readily during this cool period. If other tropical companion animals are kept in the vivarium, the minimum nighttime temperature should be 65° F, with 68–72° F being the more desirable temperature range. The daytime temperatures should be allowed to go up to standard normal range (low to mid 80s).

A female green anole uses its snout to bury an egg by creating a shallow depression underneath it.

Egg Clutches

Green anoles typically lay multiple clutches of single eggs as often as every two weeks. Anoles generally seek to lay their eggs under a piece of wood or bury them in a shallow depression in the ground.

If you are interested in raising anoles from eggs, the eggs should be removed and placed in an incubating container. Eggs allowed to remain in the vivarium where adults are maintained can result in hatchlings being eaten by the adults or other vivarium animals soon after emergence.

Incubation

Because of the low cost of most anoles, few people are willing to spend the money on designing an incubator for hatching anole eggs. An inexpensive alternative is to remove the eggs and bury them in a layer of moistened vermiculite (barely moist, specifically half vermiculite and half water by weight, which is approximately one-part water to twelve- to

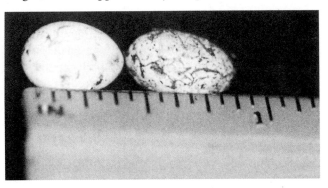

These tiny eggs are from a green anole. Green anoles will readily breed in a home vivarium if the photoperiod is properly adjusted.

fourteen-parts vermiculite, by volume) inside a small food storage container or deli container. The eggs should be buried just beneath the surface of the vermiculite. The container should be covered and a few holes punched into the cover to allow for some aeration. The container should then be placed inside the vivarium away from direct exposure to heat lamps or subsurface heat. Under these conditions, green anole eggs kept at a temperature of 84–86° F usually hatch in thirty-five to forty days.

Notice the tiny size of this knight anole hatchling.

CHAPTER 8:

CREATING A COMMUNITY VIVARIUM

One of the advantages of keeping smaller lizards is that with a large vivarium, other species of reptiles and amphibians can often be housed and displayed in the same enclosure. The general rule is to only keep together animals that are more or less of the same size and, to one's best judgment, not capable of harming or eating each other. This allows for the design of unusually interesting vivaria.

This elaborate setup contains rare and exotic plants, a miniature filtered waterfall, and various polychrid species including prehensile-tailed polychrus (*Polychrus marmoratus*).

Landscaping

A key to designing a successful community vivarium is to landscape the vivarium to divide the space into a diversity of niches. Choosing animal species that will not compete for the same vivarium niches is also critical. For example, combine semiterrestrial and arboreal anoles, small geckos (which tend to remain on the inner walls of the vivarium

or vertical slabs of cork bark), tree frogs that only become active towards the evening, and one or two tiny species of toad or possibly small terrestrial lizards. There will have to be considerable experimentation and careful monitoring in the initial set up of a community vivarium. Be careful not to overcrowd.

Quarantine

Prior to introducing any new animal to the community vivarium, the animal should be quarantined and maintained in a smaller vivarium for at least thirty days—preferably sixty days. During the quarantine period, observe the health status of the animal. Is it active? Does it feed readily? Is it gaining or losing weight? Is it gaping? Any health problems should be treated. An animal should be active, feeding well, and have good weight prior to introduction into a community vivarium. A particular concern for all herpetoculturists is avoiding the introduction of life-threatening viral diseases. Although diseases are impossible to avoid completely, quarantining animals for at least thirty days will minimize the risk of introducing them to your collection.

When possible, treat the animals for parasites during the quarantine period. In a closed system such as a vivarium, parasites with direct life cycles can increase to critical levels and eventually wipe out inhabitants of a community vivarium. In addition, certain species may be particularly susceptible to parasites of another species. Treating parasites may be easier said than done but a good reptile veterinarian should be able to help you establish both a diagnostic and treatment protocol. In time, with a basic microscope and a small amount of equipment, you should be able to identify and treat some of the more common parasites.

Animal Size

Only mix amphibians and reptiles with a snout-to-vent length (the measurement from the tip of the nose to the vent) of at least 50 percent the snout-to-vent length of the largest animal. These are broad guidelines.

Vivarium Size

Don't overcrowd. A rule of thumb for a community vivarium is that the vivarium should have a length of at least five times the total length of the largest animal, and a width of at least one and a half times the total length of the largest animal. The sum of the total lengths of all the animals in the vivarium should not exceed three-fourths the length of the vivarium. This is a broad guideline that can be somewhat exceeded in wide vivaria or if one combines animals that inhabit different niches in the vivarium, such as geckos on the walls, anoles on branches, and small toads or terrestrial lizards at ground level.

The greater scaly anole (*Anolis tropidonotus*) is from Honduras. As with most anoles, the male (above) is larger than the female.

CHAPTER 9:

NOTES ON OTHER ANOLES

At this time, relatively few anole species are offered in the pet trade other than those that can be collected in the United States. There are few longevity records kept for most species. Only the most common are usually recorded and often refer to wild-caught adults in captivity, and thus do not reflect the potential life span of a species. As a rule, smaller anoles can be expected to live five to seven years and larger ones seven to more than ten years. The following are usually available during the warmer months:

A male brown anole *(Anolis sagrei)* displays its dewlap. This species is readily available in the trade and can be kept with green anoles.

Brown Anole *(Anolis sagrei)*

This was one of the first introduced anoles to become established in south Florida. The brown anole is more terrestrial than the green anole and prefers larger resting areas (e.g., bases of tree trunks). In a well-designed vivarium, these lizards make an attractive display, particularly the males with their large orange red dewlaps.

Close-up of a brown anole.

Sexing

Males are larger than females and have larger heads. When excited, males raise a slight nuchal crest. Males have beautiful bright orange red dewlaps with a light edge.

Size

Adults reach a total length of 5 to 8½ inches. Males are larger. Make an effort to select brown anoles that are within the size range of your green anoles. A large male brown anole might find a small green anole to be a tasty morsel.

Diet

With adequate food, one or more brown anoles can be maintained with a small group of green anoles.

Breeding

Similar to green anoles, but night temperatures during the cooling period should not drop below 60° F.

Big-Headed Anole *(A. cybotes)*

This species used to be imported in some numbers from Haiti. Today, they are mostly available in small numbers as collected specimens from limited areas of south Florida where they have been introduced.

Their appeal is the relatively short but large head of males. The males also have stout bodies with generally

43

heftier proportions than found in most anoles. In habits, they are a bit like the brown anole.

Sexing
Males are larger than females. They have proportionately larger heads and a large pale yellow dewlap.

Size
Males grow up to 8 inches. Females are considerably smaller, typically around 5 inches.

Diet
All anoles are insect eaters. The larger ones will eat small lizards, including baby anoles when available. In captivity they will eat pink mice.

Breeding
Similar to the green anole, but minimum night temperature should be 65° F.

The Cuban anole *(Anolis equistris)* is the largest of the anoles, as well as one of the longest lived. These lizards will adapt to captivity if provided with a large enclosure and ample heat and humidity.

Cuban, or Knight Anole *(A. equestris)*
This species, which has been introduced and established in south Florida, is one of the outstanding anoles. Cuban anoles are impressive, display well, and, with a minimum of

care, thrive in vivaria and reproduce with some regularity. In captivity, Cuban anoles can live to ten years or more.

With some handling, young established specimens can become relatively tame, although it should be made clear that these lizards are capable of inflicting a nasty bite. They are best kept in groups of one male to one or more females.

One problem with Cuban anoles is that they will try to eat whatever moves and is small enough to fit into their mouths—so any cage mates must be of similar or slightly greater size. If annoyed, they will readily bite and possibly injure a cage mate. They are compatible with some species of equal or greater size, for example, green iguanas if kept in very large vivaria. They are not compatible with green anoles.

Sexing
Males will grow to a larger size than females. The head of males, particularly older males, is significantly more massive and its upper surface is more rugose than that of females. Hemipenal bulges at the base of tail are the best indicators of sex.

Size
Large males can reach a total length of 20 inches. This is one of the largest of the anoles. It cannot be kept with any smaller lizard, including other anoles.

Diet
Cuban anoles will eat larger prey including smaller lizards. In captivity, they will readily feed on large crickets, king mealworms, and pink to early-stage fuzzy mice.

Hatchlings have the same diet as adult green anoles. The author has observed Cuban anoles kept with a green iguana feed on plant matter, particularly ripe tomatoes.

Breeding
With decreased photoperiod in the winter and a night temperature drop to 68° F, Cuban anoles will breed readily. Females usually lay up to four clutches of one or two eggs.

Hatchlings are very attractive with white bars on the sides. Initially hatchlings may be reluctant to feed and may have to be hand-fed pre-killed insects during the first few feedings. Hatchlings tend to be delicate and should be maintained under optimal conditions.

Vivarium Considerations

Use a standard 29-gallon (30-inches-long by 18-inches-high by 12-inches-wide) aquarium with screen top. For a breeding group of one male and two females, a minimum 55-gallon vivarium is recommended. Only larger vivaria allow for naturalistic vivarium design. Cuban anoles can successfully be kept loose on houseplants and branches set in a corner of a room with spotlights for heat and light.

In naturalistic vivaria, add thicker branches both diagonally and vertically. Use larger plants such as Monstera (cut-leaf philodendron), Ficus species, and large philodendron species. Dracaena can be planted sideways to provide room for climbing.

Jamaican Anole *(A. garmani)*

This moderately large species has been recently introduced in south Florida and is now regularly offered by specialist dealers.

Jamaican anoles are very attractive but also very nervous, aggressive, and territorial anoles. They are best kept in large, well-planted vivaria. You must keep them in

Jamaican anoles must be kept in a large vivarium.

A Jamaican giant anole *(Anolis garmani)* is shown on a perch.

single pairs in large vivaria with elevated branches. Their aggressive and secretive nature limits their appeal, but in time they will come out of hiding. This species should not be handled.

They can be maintained like the Cuban anole but should not be kept with other species or other Cuban anoles of the same sex.

Sexing
Males are larger than females with larger heads and hemipenal bulges.

Size
Males grow up to 4½ inches snout-to-vent length and up to 13½ inches total length. Hatchlings are around 3 inches total length. Females are much smaller.

Diet
Diet is like that of other anoles.

Breeding
These anoles will breed year round if kept in well-lit tanks with a fourteen-hour photoperiod.

Others
Other *Anolis* species are occasionally available in the pet trade in small numbers. Recently, *Anolis* species from Guyanas and the crested anole *(Anolis cristatellus)* from Puerto Rico have become available. Anoles from Nicaragua have also been sporadically imported. There are also rumors of some of the other Cuban species becoming available one day (Cuba has some outstanding larger species).

As a rule, most *Anolis* species can be maintained under the general guidelines mentioned in this book, although they are not usually as tolerant of cool night temperatures or winter temperatures as the green anole. Careful observation of the behavior of anoles should guide you as to their requirements, for example, whether they bask or appear to avoid heat, whether they drink unusually large amounts of water, their preferred vivarium niche, and their territorial or aggressive behaviors.

A good herpetoculturist is invariably a good observer and one who can adjust the captive environment to meet an animal's essential needs.

A male Martinique anole *(Anolis roquet roguet)* shows why this species is considered one of the most attractive anoles to originate from the West Indies.

The *Anolis occulatus* is from Rosean Dominica.

The *Anolis smallwoodi palardis* is a very attractive giant anole. This specimen is from Guantanamo Bay, Cuba.

The Marie Gallante anole *(Anolis ferreus)* is from Marie Gallante, Lesser Antilles. Attractive and difficult-to-obtain anoles like this one are worth breeding in captivity.

The western giant anole *(Anolis luteogularis)* is another giant anole from Cuba.

This captive born and raised clouded anole *(Anolis nebulosa)* is from Sonora, Mexico, and was photographed courtesy of the Arizona Sonoran Desert Museum.

CHAPTER 10:

COMPATIBLE SPECIES FOR ANOLE VIVARIA

The following are some species that can be kept with adult green anoles (juveniles will be eaten by anything that can swallow them), particularly in larger, well-designed vivaria (29 gallons and up). Vivaria should be planted with a variety of vertical and horizontal shelters.

House Gecko (*Hemidactylus* sp.)

House geckos will fare well in a vivarium with green anoles as long as you avoid sharp drops in night temperature. The minimum night temperature should be 65° F.

Distribution
Southeast Asia

Sexing
Males have visible hemipenal bulges at the base of the tail.

Size
Most species are 2½ to 3½ inches long.

Diet
Similar to green anoles

Breeding
House geckos breed readily and lay multiple clutches of two eggs each.

The prehensile-tailed polychrus *(Polychrus marmoratus)* is an interesting lizard that is occasionally imported from the Guyanas. Before establishing in captivity, this species must be treated for parasites.

Flying Gecko *(Ptychozoon lionatum):*

These neat medium-sized geckos fare well with anoles only when keeping smaller flying geckos with larger green anoles or medium-sized species of anoles. Given the opportunity, larger flying geckos may find smaller anoles to be a large but quite satisfying meal.

Distribution
Southeast Asia

Sexing:
Males have pronounced hemipenal bulges at the base of the tail.

Size
Up to 6 inches total length.

Breeding
Flying geckos breed readily in vivaria laying multiple clutches of two eggs each.

Gold Dust Day Geckos *(Phelsuma laticauda)*
These beautiful diurnal geckos should be kept in single pairs or trios unless a very large vivarium is provided. They live six to eight years.

Distribution
Madagascar

Sexing
Males are slightly larger and have pronounced femoral pores.

Size
Range in size from 3 inches to 5$\frac{1}{16}$ inches.

A gold dust day gecko can be kept with an anole.

Diet

In addition to the standard insect fare, day geckos should be given banana baby food with calcium carbonate or a reptile calcium/D_3 supplement once a week. This mix should be offered in a small shallow container (such as a jar lid) placed on the ground against the wall of a vivarium.

Breeding

If maintained properly, the above day geckos will breed readily, laying multiple clutches of two eggs each.

Other Day Geckos

Several other small day geckos, such as peacock day geckos (*P. quadriocellata*) and leaf-tail day geckos (*P. serraticauda*) will fare well with anoles, but only one species should be selected and only single pairs or trios.

Pigmy Skinks *(Mabouia macularia)*

These small, attractive skinks are good companions to anoles, but only if kept in a large vivarium that does not house too many animals. They do not like excessively warm temperatures but do well at temperatures in the mid to upper 70s. They should be kept at temperatures from the mid 70s to 82° F. They require high humidity with good ventilation. Their housing requirements are similar to long-tailed grass lizards, with which they can be readily maintained. These pretty skinks are hardy, interesting little animals that tend to be secretive, frequently spending their time in shelters or burrowed in fine orchid bark, which is recommended as a ground medium.

Distribution

Southeast Asia

Sexing

Mature males are more colorful with orange on the underside of the throat, but this is not always reliable, particularly in younger males. A surefire method is to evert the hemipenes; this is easily done by holding a skink upside down in one hand while pulling back the anal plate with the thumb and with the other hand, using the thumb beginning at an area roughly ⅓ to ½ of an inch from the vent, pressing in and up toward the vent. This should be done gently. Little pressure is required to cause hemipenal eversion.

Size
Up to 3¼ inches

Diet
The diet should consist of two-to three-week-old crickets, although these skinks will feed on dead crushed larger insects.

Asian Long-Tailed Lizards, also called Asian Grass Lizards *(Takydromus sexlineatus)*
If you look at them closely, these lizards have neat little faces with intense eyes. They're interesting vivarium lizards if you can get them established.

Long-tailed grass lizards can only be kept with small companion animals. Even a large flying gecko may find a smaller long-tailed lizard a tasty treat. A lot of herps will consider them a snack and so will birds. Think before you mix.

Some of the groups of imports have poor survival rates. Besides poor husbandry, flagellate protozoans is one of the most common causes of decline in these lizards. In many imported lizards unsanitary watering methods are a primary cause of disease spread.

Distribution
Southeast China, various subspecies occur in the Malay Peninsula, Hong King, Burma, and Hainan

Sexing
The tails of males thicken past the vent and are generally markedly thicker compared to the more tapered tails of females. The difference is unmistakable. Mature males also tend to have somewhat brighter, higher-contrast coloration

The Asian long-tailed lizard *(Takydromus sexlineatus)* is an interesting lacertid that will fare well with green anoles in large vivaria. Unfortunately, imports harbor internal parasites that must be treated before introducing to a vivarium.

with the background color, which is often a darker, richer shade than that of females. The lateral stripes are cream yellow compared to the off-white of females.

Size
Up to 13 inches total length with a snout-to-vent length just under 3 inches long.

Diet
As a primary diet, two- to three-week-old crickets are a must because this species will only consume smaller insects. They will, however, feed to some degree on crushed, prekilled larger insects. A small, shallow water dish should be provided.

Breeding
Pre-breeding conditioning is similar to green anoles but the night temperature should not be lower than 65° F. Long-tailed lizards are egg-layers, laying from four to ten tiny eggs per clutch. Under proper conditions they will lay several clutches per year.

Vivarium Considerations
These elongated slender lizards of the family Lacertidae are suitable companion lizards in green anole vivaria that are not kept too warm. These lizards do well at temperatures from the mid 70s to 82° F. This species lives primarily in

grasslands and, like anoles, requires a moderately high relative humidity. However, they will not fare well in vivaria with saturated humidity and poor ventilation. A layer 1-inch thick or more of orchid bark is recommended as a ground medium. This will provide these lizards with a burrowing medium they seem to enjoy and may possibly require. A small humidifying shelter is recommended.

Green Tree Frog *(Hyla cinerea)*

This is a pretty and readily available U.S. species that lives at least five years.

Distribution
United States

Sexing
The male's throat is slightly darker (grayish, sometimes with a dirty yellow tint) than the female's, with looser skin that tends to form folds.

The spring peeper *(Hyla crucifer)* is one of several small North American tree frogs that fare well in anole vivaria. The plant is a jewel orchid *(Haemaria discolor)*. Both plant and frog make excellent long-term residents in large vivaria.

Size
1¼ inches to 2½ inches

Diet
Similar to anoles

Vivarium Considerations
Green tree frogs fare well in large (20-gallon plus), uncrowded vivaria containing anoles.

The only additional requirement is a water dish with a rock in it to allow for easy access in and out of the container. Purified water or high-quality drinking water should be used. Clean water should be available at all times.

A gray tree frog *(Hyla versicolor)* rests on the leaves of an Epidendrum orchid. This frog was photographed in the same vivarium as the spring peeper.

Other Tree Frogs and Toads
Spring peepers *(H. crucifer)* and gray tree frogs *(H. versicolor)* have also been successfully maintained in vivaria with anoles. Other small species of tree frogs would probably fare well.

If the vivarium is very large, you could probably include miniature species of toads. A shallow container of water, which you must keep clean, should be available at all times.

CHAPTER 11:

NATURALISTIC VIVARIA

This book has presented in a very general and limited manner the possibilities of designing naturalistic community vivaria for anoles and other amphibians and reptiles. There are many other landscape designs possible, as well as many other species of amphibians and reptiles that would fare well under these conditions. Stay open to experimentation in this area as long as certain basic criteria are met:

- Use a large vivarium. The larger it is, the greater the opportunities of successfully keeping several species together.
- Select small species. Larger species damage the landscape, require more space and defecate too frequently and in too copious amounts to keep a naturalistic vivarium going for very long.
- Quarantine and treat animals prior to introduction.
- Keep species together that have similar environmental requirements.
- Don't overcrowd.
- Put as much focus on the plants as on the animals. Well-planted and designed vivaria enhance the beauty of the animals.
- Monitor animals and plants daily.
- Don't hesitate to make changes, particularly when various elements of a vivarium are not working.

RECOMMENDED READING

Klingenberg, R. 1993. *Understanding Reptile Parasites.* Advanced Vivarium Systems, a line published by BowTie Press™. Mission Viejo, Calif.

Rogner, M. 1997. *Lizards, volume 1 and 2.* Krieger Publishing Company, Malabar, Fla.

Schwartz, A. and R.W. Henderson. 1985. *A Guide to the Identification of the Amphibians and Reptiles of the West Indies Exclusive of Hispaniola.* Milwaukee Public Museum.

Wilson, D.W. and L. Porras. 1983. *The Ecological Impact of Man on the South Florida Herpetofauna.* University of Kansas Publications. Museum of Natural History.

Zimmerman, E. 1986. *Breeding Terrarium Animals.* T.F.H. Publications, Inc.

About the Author

Philippe de Vosjoli is a pioneer herpetoculturist who revolutionized herpetoculture with the publication of *The Vivarium* magazine and the Advanced Vivarium Systems line of books. With over a million books in print, he is the best-selling author of more than twenty books and one hundred articles on the care and breeding of amphibians and reptiles.

INDEX